The

The Matter

Kate Innes

Mindforest
Press

The Matter

Kate Innes

ISBN: 978-1-9191930-0-7

A catalogue record for this book is available from the British Library.

Published in 2025 by Mindforest Press
www.kateinneswriter.com

Printed in Great Britain by Biddles Books

Cover Artwork: 'The Messenger' & 'Two Solitudes' by Helen Garrett www.helengarrett.com
Cover Design by macreative.co.uk
Quote from *Translations* by Bill Milner, 2009, Woodlands Press

For

Liz, Ann and Ted

Matter is clearly not one solid mass:
things diminish by degrees. Length of time
sees all things slip away until old age
withdraws them from our sight, and yet the whole
is never lessened since the particles
departing from one object make it dwindle
and adding to another make it grow,
causing the one to flourish while the other fades –
though never dwelling where they come to rest.
Interdependency of transient things
in this way constantly renews the whole.
Some nations grow, others decline
and in a little time the generations
of living creatures change, like relay runners
passing from hand to hand the torch of life.

'The Torch of Life' by Lucretius
translated by Bill Milner

Contents

Ink

Like a bud it swells
at the tip of the quill
preparing its leaves

Like a well it holds
darkness   carbon seams
innumerable lives

Like blood it must flow
for a life to continue
for a story to grow

Like a bird it sweeps
across the plain of the world
spreading new seeds

Like a word it is ground
mixed by nations   generations
fixed   but never fixed

Painting the Cave – Three Voices

I – Charcoal

The wood must change, but not to ash.
It will become between-stars black.
The fire must change, but not to smoke.
Capture it with cord and fat.
Torch-flame will make the shadows dance.

Close, child, close. Follow my steps.
The dark has jaws, the floor has fangs.
On bone-white walls, life is born
and looks at you from soft dead stone.
See here, the nose of the horse you rode,
the mane you gripped, the eyes that rolled.
I summon it with lines of coal.

II – Red Ochre

It oozes from the cliff like monthly blood.
I grind it with a hammer stone
and pack it in my pouch,
collect bird egg, cut reed.
Behind me – my child
who shows no fear,
who has grown,
now flows herself
and holds the flame.

We walk into the womb.

Inside the curved folds of the walls
she seeks the hands of others,
finds their place, splays her fingers.
But she must wait –
mix blood from raw dust, egg, spit.
Full reed against my lips,
I mark her on the stone with my breath.

Red hand binds her
to the making, to the mother.

III – Calcite

Inner earth has its own organs
and pace of creation.
The glacial seep of fossil seas
keeps tangible time.
As sand in an hourglass,
it builds its steep mountains.
As milk flows at a baby's cry,
it responds to emptiness.
Like the rain,
it joins above and below.
Like a tree,
we die while still it grows.

Inhumation

Light greets you bit by bit,
eggshell in an empty nest.
Gently, gently with just the tip,
the trowel lifts the bones
from their cold cradle.

My real work begins
while you lie resting –
limbs lax, jaw agape.
But sleep is a distant
cousin of your quiescent state,
and, in fact, I've interrupted
your task of dissolving –
of becoming.

Just a plain bronze boss
remains of the shield
that covered your heart.
Your sword – corroded, blunted.
Isotopes, not bards,
may tell your deeds.
Elements have fingerprints,
though you no longer do.

You were a man, you died.
That's all I can know,
although I take these intimacies
and meet you in my reverie,
freshly dead and quizzical.

From this earth bed
I gather you into a tray –
you who are not here,
you who will always be.

Mother Wite

Unnatural calm, last light. Mist licks
the cliff and begs the difference
between air, sea and stone.
Beneath my cloak, old feet know
the way home from my beacons.

I'll get no thanks for my service.
Strange tongues rise through the wraiths,
words gnarled, harsh as the scrape of chains.
Longboats with many oars.
Swords and spears close to shore.
Northmen beckoned by fires I lit.

We are their next meal –
new sheaths for their blades.
Our young will be torn and worn
until they beg to die.

What is my duty?
Call upon the one who made the waves
to destroy these men,
or douse the flames with my own blood?

Kindness brings consequences.
It's no better to live than die.
This earth, this stone
will house me.

When my soul is free,
I still will serve.

The Cartography of Leaving

Looking at a map, I notice

how the toes of Cornwall have just pushed off
from the rocky cliffs of Brittany

and the ball of Devon's foot has left an indent
near St Malo

and the wrinkled instep of Dorset has been hurt by
the point of Cherbourg – and Bayeux.

I see that the heel of Kent is raised to grind out a
cigarette on the streets of Calais,

but it's unclear whether the breast of East Anglia
will miss the familiar fingers of Flanders

or be glad that the space between them will
become wider than the Pacific.

I tip the map east.

But even then, if we lay down on the continent,
with Norway at our head,

would we thrash about in our dreams until we
kicked-in the peaceful face of Ireland

before we woke?

Sea Glass

If the land was dragged from under your feet,
and you smashed your anger against a ship,
and drew back your arm and threw
your grief far out into the waves,
what would you get in return?

The sea holds all in its storms.
Kneads away the sharp pain,
nibbles down the hard edges,
rubs and rubs with its relentless
particles, carving and shaping,

until you see a beacon on the beach,
shining on its own sand island,
glowing on a dull day, taking in light
and letting it play in and around
its new boundaries. Your heart –
reflective, burnished, salvaged.

Children of Daedalus

Everything came from the sea.
The first architects practised there.
Small hand-less molluscs made
their chambered spiral stairs,
and ammonites fixed
segmented armoured suits.
The nautili secreted involutes.

Now the beaches crawl
with our desultory containers,
dregs of manmade gyres
quick-marching up the sand.
An ant threads the conch shell.
Progress resists the linear.
Caught in a net of our own device,
our time under water comes again.

Clew

Shorn, washed, combed, then
teased and pinched
between finger and thumb,
then spun, spun, spun
into a spiral thin and strong

Wound tight –
like a girdle round
a woman's waist –
until your touch
unravels all

Take it underground
into that tangled darkness
Better than any sword
or telltale candle in the dark
this will be your umbilical cord

to light and life and love
I give you my word

In the month of the roses – from Linear B

First bring the wind to mix the pollen
 the flowers to make the fruit
 the men to shake the trees
 the women to sift what's fallen
 the knife to prune the branches
 the stones to grind the olives
 the weight to press the paste
 for the oil to flow
And scent it with sage – colour it with henna

Bring the clay from the river
 the skill to the potter
 the wood for the kiln
 the reeds for the ropes
 the hands to make and to hoist
Bring the bees to the blossom
 the nectar for the honey
 the honey from the comb
 the wax to make the votive

Bring giant jars for the Goddess and the People
in the month of opening roses
And call the kri-kri from the mountains
for our feasting

Eileithyia Cave

Beneath a fig tree skirted with split fruit
beneath a hillside nuzzled by goats
a stalagmite omphalos rides the darkness
The seat of the goddess of birth
is washed in milk, adorned with crocus

Appeals cling to niche and crevasse
Shadows of longing stretch and
echo through the dark arteries
Give me a baby baby baby
Kicking with life life life

May she appease the Fates
abiding in the deep fissures
in the emptiness
calling for the next tremor
the next contraction of the plates

The Third Fate – Atropos

It starts and ends with sharpened shears.
This Iron Age idea still attempts
to separate the living from the dead.
Your life – pulled from the womb,
snipped from a twisted thread of blood,
devised, measured, without a by-your-leave,
then one sharp cut and down you go.
To Hades. You live between the blades,
so be afraid and do as you are told.

But every now, cells die and cells are born.
Above the buried, grass is grazed,
wool grown, shorn, woven, eaten by the moth.
Beginnings are not clear – ends never final.
Our atoms ravel and unravel.
What falls away is always. And is near.

Final line from *The Waking* by Theodore Roethke
('The Collected Poems of Theodore Roethke',
1953, Doubleday)

Before Rosetta

Like Nile mist gathered in a petal's palm
or a girl's long hair caught in a comb
the slap of mud-bricks drying in the sun
the chaff flying up from a winnowing pan
the weight of granite on calloused hands
or the rise of waterfowl from stands of reed
Like a crocodile's nest of pulsing eggs
or hollow stones strung around the necks
of the dead
were the words of the desert's throat
before the translators began.

Louis and Lucille Armstrong visit the Sphinx, 1961

They are not alone.

At the very least there's the photographer
and traders from the Sphinx Oriental Bazaar,
boys offering smokes, sweets, tours,
and the reporters who follow them everywhere
on this State Department-sponsored trip.

The reporters ask – 'Aren't you really a spy
for Israel using scat to pass secret messages?'
Louis says – 'I got a trumpet, and I got
a young wife, and I ain't got time to fool
with none of the stuff you guys talking about.'

Louis and Lucille stand at the edge of Africa
looking west where their foremothers
were enslaved from the continent's shores.
Louis says – 'It's getting almost so bad
a colored man hasn't got any country.'

They rest by the guardian of the pyramids,
a lion-man – some say a monster.
But Louis says – 'The horn ain't prejudiced.
A note's a note in any language.'
And lifts it to his lips.

We still hear his roar.

Sphinx II – The Woman Half

Not all teeth and tits
My fangs stay behind my lips
for now
and my breast is modestly furred
I smile deep inside my hunger
knowing all about crossroads
and afterlives
the crumbling cliff
the thin blue air
Every month and every child
little deaths
only some averted
by the right answer
And I know all about the bloody
Ages of Man
having fed them all
one way or another
You assume I'll velvet my paws
can't yet imagine
how deep the puncture
You want more time
but it congeals into myth around you
and I'm still crouching here
demanding answers

Sphinx III – The Animal Half

We might long for them –
the long-abandoned fangs,
hooves, fins and claws.
The strength of four paws flexing earth.
Luxurious lick of fur
on barbed tongue,
and questioning curl of tail.

But what we desire even more
is the never before,
unfurling, lavish wings.
Beating the air, defeating
the ancient force of gravity.
Each feather comforting another
in pinioned symmetry.

No wonder songbirds sing
in endless joy of sky and wind,
and crows tilt to spill the gust,
riding high in savage weather.

Watch a hawk retract to speed
and, post-kill, its lazy thermal rise,
the spiralling play above the trees,
and realise birds are, in fact, old gods.

Our hands should build their sanctuaries.

Common Buzzard Feather

Young as it is and harried by a crow,
the hawk fletches the wind,
thinks by feeling gust and gravity.
Each stippled feather knows the drill.
Each frond grips its fellow, holds fast,
springs with surface tension.

The strike on the wing
comes from behind,
but our ragged hawk beats on,
one feather becoming
individual.

Common as leaves,
common as stars,
unhurried, it spirals,
translucent to the sun,
translating the wind.
A last flourish on rising air,
before soft fingertips
brush the ground,
as if greeting a new lover.

Dancing all the way,
with levity,
seems an uncommon
way to fall.

Carel Fabritius regards his painting *The Goldfinch* in the hours before his death in the Delft Thunderclap, 1654

It was not easy to capture you in paint,
easier perhaps with net or glue or bait.
Though tethered, you were never still
always hopping, flapping – until

another finch in nearby field began
its song of territory – or seduction.
You understood, though I could not,
and stayed motionless, but for the cock

of your scarlet face and black ink eye.
I sketched your form – it did not satisfy.
I needed to touch to understand,
but you would not accept my hand.

Then the free bird stopped its song,
and you, lord of this meagre bounded ring,
threw the swell and chime of your call
like a charmed rope from the bottom of a well.

Your beak so small, your drumming breast,
hopeful, fettered, unable to rest.
I told Mattias which pigments to grind –
I stared at your stare, the canvas primed.

Now here you are, my finished work,
bright with gold and the hope of it.
I pray you, fly into the world
as did the bird who engendered it.

Underworld

I go through my own mind
into this limbo –
mortuary of a medical institution.

I'm not shocked by what I find.
You and I had to give that up
as organs capsized one after another.

And what has happened since
is what you wanted:
Dissection – Dissemination – Instruction.

Science and Education –
your pillars of reason
against the mob.

The alcohol and cigarettes are obvious.
Fingers yellow, bent. Lungs, heart and liver –
eddies in a polluted river.

Less so the other scars –
cries unanswered, until you stopped crying.
Things that happened to boys of your age

in schools at that time.
Gradually, in the cold, what you were
is cut away, examined and discarded.

But not from me.
I remember who you are –
a stranger to yourself

perhaps no longer.
I didn't come for prophesy or direction.
My odyssey is circular, continuous.

I came to touch you one last time,
to call you *Dad,*

to be your home and let you leave it.

Adam's return

He found the gate unguarded – except by thorn –
the angel gone
Forgotten trees had dropped their fruit
and multiplied
He walked the laxened garden long
until
he found the place where soft-leaved boughs
bent low
and touched his face like a fall of hair

This was where he would lay out his days like seeds
and forget
He dragged the beams, uprights, corrugated sheets
with no help
The following week he had table and shelves –
tin bowl and cup
He brought a lilo and bag – slept well beneath
the mossy trees
and breathed in wild, untainted air

At dawn, the birds would sing their maze
of territory
And he would rise to fix the leaking roof
without a word
So here are the fruits of his Eden tree:
solitude
the hone of a wren's eye as it alights
un-numbered days

They tempt me

Autumn at the Summer Lake

This obsession with raking leaves
what does it say to the trees
in their colourful clothes
that their gifts to the musk turtle
elver or bull frog are of no value?
And what they give to the green snake
mole or firefly is of no worth?

But they remain and we do not

Yesterday we bustled dead leaves
into plastic bags
Today more fall on the lawn
on the lake
and a million drops of rain
chase them to shore

Tomorrow there'll be no one to care

Only a heron pair
gliding over grey water
into misty shadow
The rise of a perch
haloed in bright rings

while our lives lie stagnant, fallow

Yew

If you have ever entered
an ancient church at twilight
and felt time, and all its dead,
congeal in the growing shadow,

you will understand this:
it does no good to sit
at the foot of a yew
hoping for easy comfort.

It grew from poison seed
but was never young.
The twisted sinews of its bole
rise out of earth's dark core,
drawing up iron marrow
and berries of cloying blood
that still the tongue.

In churchyards it grows
like a cairn, bone upon bone.
In woods it spreads
into dimensions come and gone
while death blows by
like a passing sparrow.

It speaks no soft-leaved words.
Rather, like a hardened prophet
implacable in the market place,
it cries, 'All men are grass.'

Even so, you might stand
beneath its boughs, sheltered
like any other wary creature,
reprieved, artless, unmanned.

One Way

An old man stopped traffic on the high street,
short-shuffling into the road in front of a van,
finger raised in an arthritic question mark,
tortoise back heavy with years.

The white van waited just long enough
then flicked the indicator and passed,
flapping the black banners of his trousers,
spraying him in a fine dirty rain.

When the old man was a young man, perhaps
he drove a van – a butcher's van.
He may have overtaken an old man, thinking
Find the bone and go round it.

He may have been a quarryman, his flatbed
piled with stone. Perhaps he'd have waited
for an old man to cross the road, thinking
Find the fault and follow it.

Or maybe he never drove a van, but has walked
the whole world, crossing roads, facing drivers,
finger raised, thinking *One day, one day.*

Bone to stone. There is no other way.

Where does the black bird sing?

A man walks through the night
carrying a domed, iron cage.
Inside the cage is a bird, deep black –
black as a narrow well.
Its beak is long. Its eyes shine.
They say the bird came from the mine
where the man's father worked.
They say that in the deepest part of the night,
the bird will speak, predicting death,
as it did below.

The man walks through the night,
his father newly buried
under only six feet of earth.
The cage and its resident are heavy,
but they are his only inheritance.
An augury bird that he dreads to hear –
nonetheless it deserves more than a prison cell
and dirty air.
He walks over spoil hills, scree, concrete.
More grey towns.
And as he walks he thinks:

Where does the black bird sing?
What does the black bird know?
Where may it spread its wing?
How far will I have to go?

After the roads have run out
and there are no more towns,
the last path leads him to a valley – and a wood.
He puts down the cage and stares at tree upon tree
so tall, so close, so aware.
He has never seen a wood before
or that distant bird flying free.
It grows dark as he stands, uncertain,
and a waxing crescent moon begins to set.

Where will the black bird sing?
What can the black bird know?
When will I find hope's spring?
What more must I undergo?

But the black bird is silent,
its eyes gleaming in the dusk.
So between two oaks, over roots, ducking branches,
he goes, eyes wide for the source of sounds
echoing from trunks, calls and creaks
under his feet,
climbing over the fallen,
until he sees a stack of logs.

At its centre, he feels a gap
where a thick log should have been.
He puts the cage down and crawls inside.
Coffin-close the dead trees lie.

Black bird is this the end?
This night I'll hear your cry.
You were my only friend.
Why must you say I'll die?

With his coat wrapped tight round his shoulders
he sleeps
while night creatures go about on many feet,
and leaves begin to bud in the warming air,
for this is the first day of spring.

Branches of blackthorn, oak, rowan, beech
release their colours and down, their fingers reach.
On the forest floor, primroses unclasp,
violets unbend.
A cage cannot keep spring out or in.

The bird has opened its beak. The man hears.
In the dark pile of wood he fears the prediction
but crawls out into the morning, nonetheless,
to face whatever the bird will say.

At the bottom of the cage, black feathers are piled
and the bird, newly fledged,
glows like stained glass,
clothed in the shades of trees and flowers.

The man throws off his coat, opens the cage door
and moves back to watch.

This is the place it will sing.
This is the time it will fly.
Now it will stretch its wing.
Here I don't fear to die.

The bird bobs its head,
moves one thorny claw forward,
then the other. It is balanced on the edge,
its eye still black and bright.
It hops onto earth, tests its wings,
launches itself, circles and comes to rest
on his shoulder.

He strokes its feathers with calloused hands.
'Tell me who you are.' But the bird does not speak.
It flexes its legs and flies to the top of the oak,
where it sings. And all the forest birds answer it.

This is the place of the song.
This is the home that was lost.
This is the place we belong.
Here we may live without cost.

The man lies back on the forest floor –
eyes open, arms wide, chest rising.

I become a tree

Asleep among trees
alone – I lie on moss
I do not decay
I dissolve
become water, mineral,
seep into earth

And the one kernel of truth
inside begins unfurling
into a species unknown
throws a pattern
of light and shadow
on the forest floor

its height elusive
its depth a mystery
And whether owls
or snakes nest there
I do not know

There is no god
who will make judgment
on my character
in this metamorphosis
No rape or tragedy
forces me

When I long for rest
this is where I go
Drop to earth – lie prone
in the potent undercroft
Become upright
Breathe, fall, grow,
taste light

The Armageddon Afterparty

After lift-off – it was just a little while
before cocktails were served
in the tungsten gravity glasses
and the passengers could float and mingle
and see through the forward reinforced window
the spaceships of the other trillionaires
glinting in cold sunlight
some less, some more phallic and streamlined
and behind them the trundling cattle trucks
of robotic slaves, ready to work on arrival
at their clean, pneumatic future
No one was looking out the rear window
where a blue sphere smeared with grey smoke
and red dust grew smaller and smaller

They drank more before purging, and more again
It would be a long, long voyage
They would slingshot the moon
then sleep in luxury life-support pods

But for now, the lucky ones could toast
their future, their foresight,
that campaign of universal imperialism
that demanded sacrifice
in experiments without atmosphere
The next planet was perfect – primed
They could knock back another one

Behind them, Earth loosened her belt

Notes

Saint **Wite** (p. 16) is said to have been a Saxon woman who looked after beacons on the Dorset coast and was killed by Vikings arriving on the beach at Charmouth in the 9th century. Her early medieval shrine is still intact in the church of St Candida and Holy Cross in the village of Whitchurch Canonicorum. The shrine was opened in 1900 and found to contain the skeleton of a woman about forty years old.

In ancient Greek Mythology, **Daedalus** (p. 20), architect of the famous labyrinth, escaped from Crete by making wings for himself and his risk-taking son, Icarus. King Minos wanted Daedalus back and set a challenge to tempt him out of hiding: to thread the spiral of a conch shell. Daedalus tied the thread round an ant and put honey at the other end of the shell to tempt it.

Linear B (p. 22) is a Bronze Age written language of the Mycenean civilization from the Aegean area, including southern Greece and Crete. It was eventually deciphered by Michael Ventris in the early 1950's. Mainly used for account keeping, it also reveals fascinating details about religious beliefs and festivals.

Eileithyia Cave (p. 23) is located on the island of Crete in the Aegean Sea, behind the beach and ancient port of Amnisos, where, it is said, Zeus's umbilical cord dropped off after his birth on Mount Ida. Eileithyia was a very ancient goddess of childbirth, said to be a companion of the Fates. The cave is still adorned with offerings.

Atropos (p. 24) was the third of the triad of Fates (the Moirai) in Classical Greek Mythology. The first (Lachesis) spun the thread of life, the second (Clotho) measured it, and the third cut it. Atropos is often shown carrying a large pair of shears.

The quoted words of **Louis Armstrong** (p. 26) are taken from the following article about his trip to Egypt: https://www.vintag.es/2017/01/behind-iconic-image-of-louis-armstrong.html

Carel Fabritius (p. 30) and his student – Mattias Spoors – were killed in the explosion of the gunpowder magazine in Delft which destroyed his studio, many of his paintings, and a quarter of the city. Conservation of 'The Goldfinch' painting has shown numerous small dents which must have been formed when the paint was not yet dry, perhaps caused by the explosion.

Acknowledgements

Thanks are due to the editors of the following publications: *The New European* who published 'The Cartography of Leaving' in April 2019, *Ten Poems from Welshpool* – Candlestick Press who published 'Yew', *Whirlagust II* – Yaffle Press who published 'Adam's Return', and *Festival in a Book – A Celebration of the Wenlock Poetry Festival* – 904 Press who published 'The Armageddon Afterparty'.

'Adam's Return' was commended in The Yaffle Prize 2020. 'I become a tree' was runner up in the Cresswell Crags Nature Poetry Competition 2020. 'The Armageddon Afterparty' was the winner of the 'Festival in a Book Poetry Competition' judged by Helen Ivory and Martin Figura in 2023. 'Yew' and 'One Way' were special mentions in the Welshpool Poetry Festival Competition, judged by Di Slaney in 2023 and Helen Mort in 2025.

'Carel Fabritius regards his painting …' was displayed as part of the exhibition 'A Charm of Goldfinches' curated by Andrew Howe and Brian Eccleshall, which started in the Gateway Gallery, Shrewsbury before travelling to Sheffield and other locations.

‘Where does the black bird sing?’ was commissioned by musicians Charlotte Watson and Steve Downes (of *Whalebone Music*) as part of a DYCP Arts Council grant. Evocative ambient music was created to surround the narrative poem.

Many of the poems in this collection were written during a collaboration with visual artist Helen Garrett (www.helengarrett.com) as part of her solo show, *Primordial Dance,* at the Bridport Arts Centre November – December 2025. Work from this collaboration includes: ‘Inhumation’, ‘Mother Wite’, ‘Ink’, ‘Sphinx – The Animal Half’, ‘Eileithyia Cave’, ‘In the month of the roses’, ‘The Third Fate – Atropos’, ‘Children of Daedalus’ and ‘Painting the Cave’.

It was a privilege to work with Helen and to record ‘Inhumation’ as part of the film *Helen Garrett – Befriending the Mystery* by Artscape Productions: https://www.youtube.com/@Artscapedocs

I’m deeply thankful for a decade’s worth of advice and support from Writing West Midlands through their Room 204 Writer Development Programme.

I'm grateful for the honesty and encouragement of creative colleagues and friends – especially Helen Garrett, Liz Lefroy, Alison Lester, Deb Alma, Di Slaney, Sarah Ibberson, Rachel Freeth, Susie Stapleton, Jonathan Davidson, Jo Jackson, Andrew Howe, Pat Edwards, Jean Atkin, Charlotte Watson, Steve Downes, Mary Cunningham, Kathryn Weaver, Karen Parkes, Catherine Nelson, Karen Robinson, Lucy Armstrong-Blair, Claire Coventry, The Bleackley Family, The Streetly Family, Marc and Christine DeMarchena-Low, Rebecca Busch-Adams, Bob and Bonnie Havery and Christopher Sweeney.

I am particularly indebted to Ted Eames and Ann Mason for their wisdom, editorial expertise and encouragement. Also to Bill Milner – whose words of advice were few but powerful.

Special thanks to my tremendously supportive family of Inneses, Osborns and Rundhaugs – near and far – particularly my mum, Sonja.
And finally, huge thanks to Freya (excellent baker), Jim (expert hugger), John (sea glass giver), and Michael (ship, harbour and lighthouse rolled into one).

Books by Kate Innes

Poetry

Flocks of Words
Shortlisted for the Rubery Book Award 2018

'Innes's wide-ranging eye moves from the 'baby fists' of unfurled bracken, and beyond to the birds and stars, taking in a wider view of our place in the ancient, unchanging spaces, with a voice that is wise and musical.' **Deborah Alma**

'Kate Innes creates extraordinarily rich, well-crafted poems, at the same time managing to retain a rare delicacy of touch ...This is landscape poetry at its best.'
Pauline Prior-Pitt

Adult Fiction

The Arrowsmith Trilogy:
The Errant Hours
All the Winding World
Wild Labyrinth

Children's Fiction

Greencoats – Rubery Book Award Shortlisted 2022

An Ancient Haunting – *Lily Ash Book One*